—A TRIBUTE TO JOHN LENNON—

A TRIBUTE TO JOHN LENNON
1940-1980

PROTEUS BOOKS
London and New York

PROTEUS BOOKS is an imprint of
The Proteus Publishing Group

United Kingdom
PROTEUS (PUBLISHING) LIMITED
Bremar House,
Sale Place,
London W2 1PT

United States
PROTEUS PUBLISHING CO., INC.
distributed by
THE SCRIBNER BOOK COMPANIES, INC.
597 Fifth Avenue
New York, N.Y. 10017

ISBN 0 906071 80 1

First published in U.K. 1981.
First published in U.S. in 1981.
© 1981 by Proteus Publishing Co., Inc.

Edited by Lyn Belanger, Michael Brecher,
Jo Kearns, Nicolas Locke, and Mike Shatzkin

Design and Production by Celie Fitzgerald

Jacket illustration by J. P. Tibbles

Printed and bound in the U.S.

INTRODUCTION

Publishing a book aimed at the members of the John Lennon community most likely to be offended by the exploitation of his name requires some explanation.

A Tribute to John Lennon was written by about 75 people in the moments of painful introspection and self-examination that followed his death. Searching through everything written since then you can find any perspective imaginable. There really isn't a category of humanity John Lennon doesn't touch.

Between the mass of words and this book was a selection process administered mainly by consensus. The mass is much more like Lennon than the book is. Omitted as much as possible are references to the circumstances of his death, reports of times he was in a surly mood, and the criticism that this person or that has of Paul, George, Ringo, or Yoko. That kind of thing doesn't belong in this book because that kind of thing is true of all of us; this book is about why John Lennon is special.

We at Proteus hadn't discussed *why* he was special until the middle of December of 1980. But we never disagreed. First of all—always first of all—is the music: a legacy so rich from a 40-year-old man that you wonder how he had time to do anything else. But of course, he did *everything* else: wrote books, made movies, helped make a family, kept a house, treated the people he loved with respect, consistently opposed violence, said what he thought, kept his priorities straight. The richness of John Lennon's life is something that we feel and understand better than the people after us will feel and understand. We were part of it.

All of us considered the moral conflict in using our professional skills on the back of somebody else's name and reputation. We are glad that *The Spirit Foundation* and *Handgun Control, Inc.* both agreed to accept royalties from the sale of this book. The people who permitted us to reprint their pieces (gratis, except where some bureaucratic requirement made it easier to pay a token fee) knew that. Some omissions resulted from rights not granted; we were sorry to lose the pieces but we respect the dilemma.

Our mission in creating this book was to bind the moments of many inspirations—all generated by Lennon's own inspiration—into a unit of some lasting value. "Then we will remember things we said today."

M.S.
for Proteus Publishing

—A TRIBUTE TO JOHN LENNON—

THIS IS ALL ABOUT THE JOHN LENNON I LOST

Denny Boyd, Vancouver Sun, Canada, December 11, 1980

To me, and others of my age, Lennon was more than a voice and a writing talent. He was a Time. I believe that the western world was close to a cultural and moral renaissance in the '60s. Your generation almost made it, Jamie, but mine stopped you. You wanted peace and honesty, but we forced you to take war and deceit. That's the broad part of the reason why I long for the Sixties, the time of flowers, the Beatles, the magnificent period songs of Paul Simon and Art Garfunkel.

The other part is more personal. I blew the Sixties. During that decade of such glittering promise, I didn't hear the music or the message in time.

Like so many of my generation, I was full of fears and doubts and failures in the Sixties, and out of a smothering sense of apprehension I forced my five little children to share them with me by association.

I remember watching my children watching the Beatles on television and the curious dichotomy of reaction within me. I admired the lovely cheek of the lads, but I wanted my kids to show more respect. I hated the haircuts, but admitted that I hadn't heard music *move* like that since Count Basie's rhythm section. The beauty of the Lennon-McCartney lyrics touched me, but where would they lead my kids? To free love? To drugs? To the Road?

You see, for my generation, the Sixties was not a time to trust anyone. Kennedy promised us Camelot, but he lied about the Bay of Pigs before another madman blew him away. Johnson lied about the Tonkin Gulf and, like other old men before him, supported an unjust war to be fought by young men.

Kent State was the ultimate, horrific lie, one generation slaughtering another in the shame and sham of national security.

I spent the mid-Sixties worrying that my children would be corrupted by drugs, and I finished the decade drinking two quarts of gin a day.

That's why, lately, I have been trying to rediscover the Sixties that went by while I was distracted.

There is a Burt Reynolds movie, in which he plays a weary, burned-out detective. He has a failed marriage behind him, a dirty murder case on his hands and no bright prospects out front. Someone says to him: "You must miss your ex-wife." He thinks about it and says, with great weariness: "No, I miss Artie Shaw." For some, it is a flippant remark. For others it holds aching meaning, the longing for another time.

I was born after the Jazz Era, grew up in the middle of the Big Band Era. I will always love jazz. But jazz merely excites my nerve endings, it never has and never will enrich my soul or my mind. But Lennon, McCartney, Simon and Garfunkel, they gave my children not just rhythm, but words with meaning.

I listen to a lot of music, and in the last six months the single album I have been playing over and over again is The Best of Simon & Garfunkel. It is the closest I can come to hearing the Sixties that my vision never totally absorbed.

Byron never wrote a better love poem than Simon's To Emily, Whenever I Find Her. The Sound of Silence might be the 11th Commandment Moses forgot: Thou Shall Not Be Passive. Could there be a more beautiful blessing than, "Your time has come to shine, all your dreams are on their way. See how they shine!"

The songs of the Beatles and of Paul Simon were songs of searching and optimism, a search for something believable in a time of disbelief. That faith of the Sixties was rewritten in the late Seventies by lesser talent to read: "I know I seek perfection in a quite imperfect world and fool enough to think that's what I'll find." Quite a difference in perspectives, in one decade.

John Lennon was a contradictory man, from the stridency of his search for religious belief to the snowflake gentleness of the man who could write Imagine.

I don't believe he was as complicated as his cultists painted him. He wrote a song called Lucy in the Sky with Diamonds. His cultists took the L, the S and the D and believed Lennon had slickered everyone by putting a song about LSD on the radio. The truth was quite different and indicative of the essential Lennon. His son Julian, now 17, came home from school and made a stick drawing of a little girl looking at a sky filled with childishly-drawn stars. "Who's that, son?" Lennon asked. The little boy said: "This is my friend, Lucy." Lennon wrote a song about Lucy and her sky filled with diamond stars, a father showing pride in the small piece of art his child had created.

I admire Lennon for doing that.

My generation told lies to the Beatles' generation, but the Beatles never lied to my kids. They gave them Strawberry Fields and promised them There Will Be an Answer.

I thank John Lennon for giving my kids words to enjoy and dreams to chase at a time when I was not often around or capable enough. He took them and kept them for a while and he gave them back to me, unharmed and still full of love for me.

That is the John Lennon I lost.

"YESTERDAY" MOURNING BEFORE SUNRISE

*Richard Roberts, The Evening Bulletin, Philadelphia, PA,
December 10, 1980*

I am 32 years old—I grew up during the Age of the Beatles. I can remember in early 1964, when I was 15 years old, calling a local disc jockey and dedicating the Beatles' first big hit, "I Want to Hold Your Hand," to my girlfriend. I later married her.

The Beatles seemed to fill the music needs of our generation. They captured the mood. As we grew older, wiser and more sophisticated, so did they. They led the way with lighthearted songs; through their deep and serious inter-reflection on themselves and the world around them; and finally emerging as profound, serious and accomplished musicians, songwriters and true poets of our time. And if Paul McCartney was the heart of the Beatles, John Lennon was their soul and the spokesman for youth.

I remember the shock and sense of loss when the Beatles finally broke up. It seemed the passing of an era. It was like entering adulthood or learning that Santa Claus was not real. You knew that they, like you, had to move on, but you felt you were leaving something behind.

One consolation was that at least we could still enjoy the individual music of John Lennon, Paul McCartney and Wings, and on occasion, George Harrison and Ringo Starr. And, as though to fill our own secret needs, there would surface the rumors that the "Four from Liverpool" would reunite just one more time.

Over the last several years Paul McCartney kept alive our musical love affair with the Beatles, but John Lennon kept alive our conscience. He was our justification in still holding on to their old songs. Here he was, with Yoko Ono, searching for his family roots in trying to win custody of his child, fighting to stay in the U.S. because New York and our way of life represented the ultimate in the Western World's joining of art, music, literature, technology and all of creativity rolled together.

He lent his name and his money to fighting drug abuse and helping disabled and disadvantaged children and striving for a better world. Just a few months ago, he donated money to the New York City Police Department for bulletproof vests; ironically, he was assassinated by an assailant who shot him in the chest. John Lennon's life was snuffed out at a time when he had just released a new album, with Yoko Ono, after an absence of several years.

It is different. It has a new style, a new format, a new beat and a new message. Yet it is unmistakably John Lennon. One song is called "Starting Over," and at a very bleak time as the world trudges on, it is another message to help us along. As Soviet troops mass on Poland's border, as the Iran debacle drags on and as inflation takes a new turn and interest rates soar, John Lennon came through for us again. To be sure, it was not a major or perhaps even significant contribution—certainly not of the magnitude to change anything in the world. But it did add something in our own personal lives—the flicker of that light we all keep lit because we believe that tomorrow will inevitably be better than yesterday—eternal optimism.

Another era has passed. My link with my idyllic, fanciful teen years, the ones that always seem to mold us and have the greatest meaning in our lives as we experience growing up, has ended. Another peacemaker has been taken from us and the Beatles' classic "Yesterday" takes on a new meaning—"Yesterday, all my troubles seemed so far away. Now it looks as though they're here to stay. Oh, I believe in yesterday."

Maybe I'm making too much of one person's death. But then the death of every person, every ideal, every wish, every dream should affect all of us.

It's 2 o'clock in the morning, and I just had to tell someone.

HOW JOHN WAS OVERWHELMED BY LIFE AND DEATH

Phil Sutcliffe, Northern Echo, Darlington, England,
December 10, 1980

I loved John Lennon... simple as that.

Why? Because he gave us so much and, oddly for a man who is said to have died with a fortune worth more than £100m. he asked for nothing in return. Really nothing.

From January 1963, when Please Please Me hit number one, there was so much Beatles in the air, on radio and TV and in the newspapers, that even if you couldn't afford a record player you got the beat in your blood.

That is what happened to me. The Beatles set fire to my life. Until I was 15 I was just going through the emotions of being a boy, passing in orderly fashion through the educational system, the landmarks of my life in gold stars and percentage points.

Then came the Beatles and I woke up. I became young, instead of a tame carbon copy adult, began to discover my individuality. The Beatles started a whole generation growing up instead of growing along.

So when it came to heart and soul music John opened the door for both the beat boom and Tamla Motown invasion of Black sounds. A splendid time was guaranteed for all, as he wrote in Mr. Kite, and I seem to remember spending most of the mid-Sixties with a big grin on my face.

On the other hand, 1963 was also the year of President Kennedy's assassination. As a politician he may be severely criticised now, but as an inspiration to humanity he has been unique in my 33 years. He voiced hopes for peace and understanding in a way which captured the imagination of the same people who were listening to the Beatles.

The mood chemistry of the time meant that the ideal was not allowed to die with him, and rock was to become its most convincing voice. In America Dylan's protest songs led the way.

Over there the Beatles, with the acerbic mind of Lennon at the helm, began an extraordinary voyage of discovery through political and philosophical ideas previously well beyond the pale for working class youth.

Sure I loved them as a gang, all of them. But Lennon was the one. Paul was ineffably nice as we would all like to be; George was vulnerable, as we all felt sometimes, and Ringo gave us hope that wildest dreams come true.

They were our brothers—though in saying that I suddenly realise how different a boy's feelings were from the screaming girls who thronged their concerts. Yeah, they must have been dishy, too.

But John. He made it bite.

He was the change. Before the Beatles pop had essentially been a load of tat foisted on the youth of the nation by Tin Pan Alley hacks who thought they could control and exploit the situation forever. The Beatles kicked them where it hurts.

They were ordinary working class lads who showed that anybody could write songs. Playing their own material they proved pop could be a medium worth any amount of care, passion and commitment.

In doing so they took possession of it in a spiritual sense which has continued and is ultimately more important than the ownership of the business side by giant corporations like the Beatles' own EMI.

And Lennon gave the group that backbone. As his subsequent development with Wings demonstrates, McCartney alone would not have been so very different from pre-Beatles drips like Mark Wynter, Craig Douglas and, indeed, early 60s Cliff Richard.

Paul was a great rock and roll singer, but his writing was mainly the softer stuff such as She Loves You.

Lennon had his tender side and wasn't afraid to show it from I Wanna Hold Your Hand through to Julia on the White Album or later solo pieces like Imagine, but usually his approach was tougher, more cynical and more profound.

For him young love wasn't just daft, it was hard, sexual and deep. His performance of the American R and B classic torch song You Really Got a Hold on Me, on the With the Beatles LP stood your hair on end with the strength of its emotion.

Lennon knew, respected and expressed your feelings—and pop leapt the generation gap.

Arthur Askey and Eric Sykes got their cards from Juke Box Jury and Ready Steady Go took over on TV. The business moguls stopped condescending to musicians and fans and started to be just a little bit afraid.

Under the spotlight of world media attention they experimented with drugs, the Maharishi's transcendental meditation, the co-operative business venture of Apple and radical politics.

Particularly after meeting Yoko Ono, Lennon began to stand rather apart from the rest of the group and extend his arguments into the anarchic art forms of which she was already a notorious practitioner.

In the name of peace he appeared with her in Austria entirely shrouded in a black bag on the cover of the album Two Virgins stark naked and in Amsterdam conducted a so-called "bed-in," always using his fame to project ideas into the news.

He made deliberately inflammatory statements. He said he was more famous than Jesus Christ and Klu Klux Klanners in the States burned him in effigy. Without being an intellectual he has a dynamic instinct for shocking people into thought. He could make common sense of surrealism.

Lennon's music became more and more militant moving through the uncertainties of Revolution on the B side of Hey Jude to the absolute statements of Give Peace a Chance and Power to the People.

Of course, all of this public exposure put an enormous strain on him and it's true that his significance faded in the early 70s.

His last record, apart from his recent successful but ill-conceived comeback, was Rock and Roll released in 1975, a conscious return to his roots with thunderous cover versions of the golden oldies which originally inspired him.

He withdrew into the hermitage of his New York apartment with Yoko and their child and by all reports was a very happy man living in quiet domesticity while the tide of royalty wealth flowed his way at the rate of £5m. a year.

There is no logical way his position and his death could be squared with his political beliefs, yet I don't feel disillusioned with him and I wouldn't call him a hypocrite.

He merely bowed to the inevitable or was overwhelmed by it more likely.

Over the years he gave away, squandered and was defrauded out of millions. But success on his scale in our society is rewarded by oceans of money and eventually he stopped fighting it, laid back and floated along.

What matters is what he gave. Thank you John.

LEGACY OF LENNON

Opinion, Daily Express, London, December 10, 1980

John Lennon was the musical analogue of President Kennedy for a world to whom popular music means far more than politics.

With the Beatles, he uplifted a whole generation, helping them break through the low cloud barriers of their frustrations to a universe of limitless possibilities— *"There's nothing you can do that can't be done. Nothing you can sing that can't be sung."*

And the journey he undertook was that of the youth of his time—a journey through drink, drugs, permissiveness and meditation not for their own sake, but in the hope of finding enlightenment, of finding meaning in a mad, mad world, daily creating more and more instruments for its own destruction.

He was a Pied Piper, leading kids not to a premature end but, hopefully, a belated beginning. His anthem "All You Need Is Love," is so simple in its lyrics yet zeroed straight in on the lonely anguish of a lost, bewildered generation.

John Lennon was awarded the MBE for, in Sir Harold Wilson's words, "getting kids off the streets." He voiced what they felt but could not express. His songs were something for them to cling to.

It was only natural that he later returned his honour in protest at the Biafran and Vietnam wars. They were as incomprehensible to him as to the rest of his generation. "Give peace a chance," he plaintively sang for us all.

John Lennon was too in the line of great English eccentrics —at times engaged in the bizarre; at others, in the downright potty.

But there was always, somewhere, a delicious streak of humour, especially when the media took him far more seriously than he did himself. Not for nothing was he a devoted admirer of Noel Coward.

Though he chose latterly to live in New York, a source of energy which inspired him to start over once again, he was as English as they come—fondly quoting Churchill's cheeky dictum: "It is an Englishman's inalienable right to live wherever he likes."

But to say that Lennon and McCartney were to the England of the 1960s what Gilbert and Sullivan were to the 1880s is far too narrow and simplistic. The ripples of the Beatles' musical genius, of their inimitable Liverpudlian sound, with its sometimes sensitive, sometimes surrealistic, sometimes satirical lyrics rush out, out, out—washing the shores of all continents, not just those that speak their language.

Age shall not weary him now. But there never really was any chance that John Lennon would grow old. Like Kennedy, he had that fateful youth about him. And, in the minds of all of us, he will remain not just a nostalgic reminder of our lost times and selves but more, much more—a living symbol of feelings that are forever real.

In the words of Dorothy Parker about another English eccentric: "There was never a place for him in the ranks of the terrible, slow army of the cautious. He ran ahead, where there were no paths."

Billboard, Los Angeles, CA, December 20, 1980

Frank Sinatra says: "It was a staggering moment when I heard the news. Lennon was a most talented man and above all, a gentle soul. John and his colleagues set a high standard by which contemporary music continues to be measured."

THEY LOVED HIM, YEAH, YEAH, YEAH

Leon Taylor, Ledger, Columbus, GA, December 11, 1980

John Lennon was never short on shortcomings. Even at 40, he seemed to need a comb, a razor, and a pair of jeans that had not been anointed in Pennzoil. Both his voice and his poetry were reedy. He was never as lyrical as Dylan, as smooth as Sinatra, as pretty as Liberace. Indeed, he was only the best rock singer in the world; and his death was merely a death in the family.

Lennon so shaped the mind of a generation that if you were a member of it, or just a believer in it, you felt the buck of the bullet, too. He was a man for all seasons, and his music captured all the shifts in the weather of youth. For puppy love, he and Paul McCartney wrote "I Want to Hold Your Hand." For canine lust, "Why Don't We Do It in the Road?" For the angry, "Helter Skelter." And for the lonely, "Yesterday."

Those alone are reasons to grieve. But what raised Lennon's death from irony to tragedy was that he had outgrown being young; in the much-feared middle years, in the much-despised conventional life, he had found happiness. To those who never trusted anyone over 30, his last album was a message that age was nothing to fear, that discovering the kitchen and children was like starting over. And before it really started, it was over.

When he held the stage, he made a decade seem as brief and internecine as New England spring. He set to song the time of our lives, the life of our times; and when we woke Tuesday to that burst of iron and blood, suddenly, the conspiracy we shared in being young lost its savour.

LENNON REMEMBERED FOR MORE THAN MUSIC

Russ Christian, San Jose Mercury, San Jose, CA, December 18, 1980

As I write this it has been two days since John Lennon was shot and killed. I still feel a sense of loss unlike anything I have ever experienced before in my life. The taking of the life of a man such as John Lennon is a crime for which there is no suitable justice.

John Lennon was a major influence on my life. He shaped my attitudes toward life and toward everyday dealings with life. I know that he will be remembered for his unparalleled contribution to music, but also, and perhaps, more important, I hope he will be remembered for his contribution to peace, equal rights and civil rights. If we all could have had John's attitude toward others, this world would be a much better place to live in.

I mourn for him, indeed I may always mourn for him in my heart—but not for his death, but for the contributions to the world he will never make.

President Jimmy Carter, December 9, 1980

John Lennon helped create the music and the mood of our time.

His spirit, the spirit of the Beatles—brash and earnest— was ironic and idealistic all at once.

In the 1960's John Lennon and the Beatles captured the imagination of the world. In the songs he composed he leaves an extraordinary and permanent legacy.

I know I speak for many millions of Americans when I say I am saddened....

His work as an artist and musician was far from done.

WITHIN HIS MUSIC

Richard Dyer, The Boston Globe, Boston, MA, December 14, 1980

Certain days in history change our lives and define what it is like to be a citizen of the world in our time. Most of those days that we usually talk about are the ones of national and international political tragedy, and the way we talk about them asserts both our individuality and our place in the world community surrounding us. People of my parent's generation can all still tell you what they were doing when the news of Pearl Harbor came; people my age remember what they were doing when they learned of the assassination of John Kennedy, and how at that moment they became part of a fellowship of loss.

Tuesday we learned of the murder of a singer and a songwriter, and for an entire generation, at least, this too was a defining event, the end of a relationship that had meant much to millions and another abrupt signal of the perilous conditions of existence we all live within.

The reason this was so was that John Lennon had given us so many occasions of joy, and that is what I have been thinking about since Tuesday.

One of the defining days for a significant proportion of the population was June 2, 1967, the day that "Sergeant Pepper's Lonely Lonely Hearts Club Band" was issued in America—I imagine most people between the ages of 30 and 40 can tell you what they were doing that day and can claim that all the afterwards were different because of it. Many were standing in lines waiting for the record stores to open; many more kept their radios on. And everyone was talking about the album.

I remember that I was at an end-of-the-school-year party to celebrate, of all arcane things, several friends' having passed their PhD. orals. But for once the conversation at the party wasn't about teachers and students and books you should have read and hadn't; it was about Rita the meter maid, and Mr. Kite, and Lucy in the Sky and the joys of getting to be 64 after a life full of days. The record was played over and over again at the party, and the next day I went out and bought it—it was my first rock album.

Of course by that time the music of the Beatles was everywhere, and whether or not you were a fan of rock music it was associated with your life—it was there when you met people, it was there when you broke up, and it was there when you were having a good time. Some of it was mindless noise— that was its attraction; some of it was articulating what you thought and giving voice to what you were feeling; the best of it, represented by "Sgt. Pepper," was doing what all significant art does—it was out there ahead of you, anticipating and educating what you thought and what you felt, and making you feel good while it was happening.

John Lennon wrote words and, though he cheerfully admitted that he never could learn to read music, he knew how to find out musical tunes. Because he was John Lennon the words and music immediately and automatically became something else—a political statement, a sociological phenomenon, a source of controversy and, for many, a further turn in a continuing, highly personal conversation. He lived a life of allegory, really, right up through the end. He embodied one of the central myths of Western society, the rise from humble origins to unimaginable wealth, popularity and influence. His interests began personally, with the problems of puppy love; they then turned outwards in sympathy toward the victims in society and in anger against the conditions that created the victims; they half-created, half-reflected many of the dominant fads and interests of our time—the fascination with Oriental sounds and Oriental thought, the experimentation with drugs; they reached out to international problems of the widest scope; and they ended back at the center, in the love of individuals bonded into a family.

A treacly radio commentator said the other night that "John Lennon was the Beatle all of us wanted to be." But in actual fact he was the most restless and searching of the Beatles, the one who it would have been least comfortable to be. Lennon's audience resisted most of the changes in his life and work; the public wants its entertainers to keep on doing the same things they always have, because if those things don't change, we can stop thinking we have, at least for a moment. It's almost impossible to believe now, but the first important review even of "Sergeant Pepper," the one in the New York Times, was negative, and most of the rock press who have been clotting the airwaves with eulogy the last few days had resisted every turn in Lennon's career—and most particularly all the ones in the post-Beatles period, his uncomfortable forays into the world of the conceptual avant-garde as represented by his wife, Yoko Ono, his highly politicized music, his recent celebrations of domesticity, most of all his refusal to want to be a Beatle again ("I was the walrus, but now I'm John"). In that, as in so much else, Lennon was out ahead of his admirers; he knew that the Beatles were youth, and that there is no spectacle more ridiculous and pitiful than the attempt of middle-age to be what it used to be.

Because the words and music of Lennon became so all-pervasive, and because they so rapidly became something else quite beyond mere songs, it is in a sense difficult to get back to them—though thanks to the records they are still *there*. The striking thing about listening to Lennon in the memorial tributes and on the albums old and new is how easily he triumphs over all the cliches about him. Of course his most famous lyrics are on an extraordinary level of verbal sophistication not heard in popular music since the great theater lyricists of the '30s, but the fascinating thing about the earliest songs— some of which are represented even on the final Beatle LP, "Let It Be"—is the way he can restore energy and meaning, through music and intensity of delivery, to the semi-articulate language of daily life ("You'll never know how much I really care"). The most worldly of the Beatles, the cheekiest and most satirical gave us "Dear Prudence," one of the loveliest of all popular evocations of innocence; the most eloquently angry of the rockers, the "Walrus," wrote and composed "Julia," a song of love for his mother; the wittiest of the Beatles was also the most direct in the expression of naked, autobiographical feeling.

The music is usually discussed in terms of the amalgamation of influence in it—the influence of black music, especially the blues, of Presley, of Dylan, of Chuck Berry, of the songs of the British music hall, of cabaret tunes, songs and sentimental ballads, even of Hollywood schmaltz ("Goodnight"). But what is significant is that it is always a highly *personal* amalgamation, at once instinctive and intelligent, and that most musically literate persons could tell you, if they didn't know already, which Beatles songs are really chiefly by Lennon and which chiefly by McCartney (only the earliest songs were actually jointly composed, though most of the later ones were jointly credited). The music has been compared to Schubert in its melodic freshness and invention; and in the current Playboy interview Lennon is still hooting at the analysis of "Aeolian cadences" in the London Times that set off a whole explosion of technical-musical analysis.

The new edition of Grove's Dictionary of Music and Musicians, the standard world reference book, grants 2½ columns to the Beatles, about the same as Leoncavallo, the composer of "Paglicacci" gets. (Dale Cockrell's article points out the "verbal play, irony, satire, pessimism and even grotesqueness, fitted to dense, pounding music" in Lennon's "Run for Your Life"; and of another song he writes "Many later developments in rock can be traced to Lennon's "Tomorrow Never Knows," with its constant rhythmic pattern in the drums and bass guitar; its tambura pedal point serves as a static foundation for the surrealist poetry, tape collage effects, and electronic tone-modulations".)

Many of Lennon's fans will find this intrinsically absurd, though it is certainly less so than the kind of scanning of the lyrics for "hidden" meaning that is a national pastime of the cultists; the most extended musical analysis of Lennon's work, Wilfred Mellers' "Twilight of the Gods," is actually a very acute and perceptive and helpful work that simply points out that many of the devices that Lennon used to wrench our feelings have a name and a history and that they are a part of what we experience when we listen.

What very few people have talked about in these days of eulogy—and before—is what Lennon actually *sounded* like, for his work was never simply a set of scrawlings and scratchings on a page but always also a specific realization in sound; hundreds of other performers sing Beatles songs and a few sing Lennon's later work, but all of them are surrounded by an echo larger than they are. One of the initial reasons for the success of the Beatles was that they sounded good together, that their voices were a direct reflection of the ways their personalities complemented each other—George's voice, slightly opaque, the ideal supporting sound for filling out a harmony; Ringo's voice, a bit lower than the others, uncultivated in timbre, dangerously teetering on the edge of pitch, and somehow therefore sounding sincere; Paul's elegant light high tenor, easily veering off into falsetto; and John's high baritone, grainier than the others, with more edge and grit, its American black inflections counterweighted by the Liverpudlian accent. John's voice could bounce along in simple harmony with Paul's; it was interesting how when he sang in unison with Paul it sometimes sounded like one voice, one more complete than either alone, innocence and experience allied. In the post-Beatles period Lennon's voice developed still further, partly as the result of further exposure to the Oriental sound of Yoko Ono's ululant singing and its connections to the world of avant-garde wordless vocalism and his further assimilation of black singing and gospel shouting ("Mother").

The day of the much criticized new album, "Double Fantasy," may yet come, for in it Lennon takes up McCartney's subjects but with his own tough-mindedness, and his voice, alone and in duet with Yoko's, is everything the two voices used to be—paradise regained after innocence has been tested but not restored by experience.

These are the things that will remain. The memory of

Beatlemania will fade; the photos of the weeping teenagers screaming in the aisles will look as funny as the pictures of the ancestral teenagers listening to Sinatra in the Paramount Theater. The meaning of Lennon's life and the meaninglessness of his death will be something to read about in the textbooks, and all of the accumulated baggage of the Beatles songs and the Lennon songs will drop away. What will still be there will be words and music. And for future generations, that will be enough.

THE LIGHTER SIDE OF JOHN LENNON

Don Short, Los Angeles Times Syndicate, December 14, 1980

I'm going to miss John Lennon. His voice and his music will live on, but a lot of fun and wackiness has gone out of the world:

—Like the time when he bought his first Rolls Royce and painted it in brilliant psychedelic colors. "Rolls Royces are so dull. They need cheering up!" he explained.

—Like the time he ordered a drink in his Spanish hotel and climbed into a huge plastic bubble to confuse the waiter who was coming through the door. Winked John, "This will be worth watching. How do you reckon he's going to get the drink in my hand?" He didn't.

—Like the time in St. Tropez when he bought a peak cap and started a fashion epidemic. Back in the same shop a year later he quipped with a bland face, "I've called for my commission."

—Like the time in San Francisco when fans rioted. "Where," asked John laconically, "is the fire escape?"

LENNON: ALWAYS UP FRONT

Tony Kornheiser and Tom Zito,
Washington Post, Washington, DC, December 10, 1980

Lennon was the key to the cultural phenomenon that was The Beatles, and the key to Lennon was his rebellious desire always to go beyond the norm, always to push the limits outward. To create a new style, a new ethic. It went far beyond the hair, into the psychedelic era of hallucinogenic drugs, into the contemplative era of transcendental meditation, into the passive and ultimately active resistance of the anti-war movement during the Vietnam era.

And always at the point, there was Lennon. Lennon with the smoked glasses. Lennon with the sage's beard. Lennon with the puns and pornographic drawings. Lennon with the curious Japanese woman. Lennon in the bed and in the bathtub, singing for peace and wondering why everyone else wasn't naked and singing, too. And finally, in the late '70s, Lennon, the reclusive househusband who withdrew from the music scene completely.

Undoubtedly, psychologists could have a field day with Lennon. His father had abandoned the family early. Too poor to raise her son on her own, his mother had entrusted him to an aunt and uncle. Later, he would sing about his loneliness and ultimate reconciliation with his family—a theme that colored much of his work.

Perhaps in that history is a clue to his later appeal to a generation of loners, who could sympathize with his keen sense of futility and despair and his eternal message that only reason and humor could tide one through the ubiquitous tough times on life's way.

His wit could be subtle in a raise of the eyebrow and a twinkle in the eye. It could be quick: "On this next number, those in the cheap seats please clap. The rest of you can rattle your jewelry." And it could be snide: "When I feel my head start to swell, I just look at Ringo and know we're not supermen."

Like Groucho, he knew the value of never taking one's self too seriously.

INTELLECTUAL LENNON: SOCIAL REVOLUTIONARY

Clive Barnes, Sun-Times, Chicago, IL, December 14, 1980

Lennon was one of the pacemakers of the 20th century. He made changes in our behavior, in our attitudes and thoughts. As a guiding light, along with Brian Epstein, manager of the Beatles, he, together with Paul McCartney, created a social revolution.

His voice in its time was the voice of youth all over the world. It was the voice of freedom over the chasms of generation gaps. It was also the voice of the blue-collar oppressed trying to find its way into the new, technological society.

History is going to have to record Lennon's gift not only to the world of music, but to the world itself. He, and his partner McCartney, certainly moved music in a slightly different direction. It could have been said the music during the mid-'30s had the choice of following either Arnold Schoenberg or Kurt Weill. Music followed, many would say mistakenly, Schoenberg, and it was the Beatles who put music back on the Weill track. And Lennon knew what he was doing.

Lennon was an intellect without being an intellectual— which mentally is the stylish way to go. He was funny, he was sweet and he was generous. In his mid-career, he had certain problems with drugs, but he battered those away into a new and humorously aware vision of the world. He was the iconoclast of the '60s, and, more than anyone else, he marked out that area in green paint. He was an apostle of freedom. A man of infinite delicacy.

EVERYONE SHOULD SPEAK LENNON'S LANGUAGE

Rabbi Marcus Kramer, Staten Island Advance, Staten Island, NY, December 19, 1980

The mourning of old-time fans who screeched their response to the violent rhythms of rock and roll and Beatlemania now have added hundreds of thousands to their ranks.

We who are of an older generation also mourn—we mourn the loss of a decent, creative man, a husband, a father, who chose to live among us. We may be affected now with a twinge of conscience because we spurned the music of the young and their enthusiasms.

Unfortunately, the elder citizens did not stop long enough to listen to and to comprehend, the increasing number of beautiful ballads that touched the heart. People spoke of a generation gap, of a schism between fathers and sons, between mothers and daughters. Youngsters judged wayward or law breakers were treated harshly. Many are still in the jails of countries all over the globe.

The demonstrations and vigils in memory of John Lennon have revealed very clearly what our young people have in mind. First, they are showing respect for high character, for a man of honest and straight forwardness! Second, they are delivering a message inscribed on the placards they carried. One read "Give Peace a Chance." Two: "All You Need Is Love." They want the language of peace to be seriously considered in the halls of authority.

The language of peace does not have too many exponents in the history of literature, except for the notations in the Bible. Best known is the seal of the threefold Aaronic blessing: "The Lord lift up His face to Shine upon thee and give thee peace." Equally inspiring is Psalm 29:11: "The Lord will give strength unto His people; the Lord will bless His people with peace." The Rabbis summarized the quest for peace in the words of Rabbi Simeon ben Gamaliel: "The world depends on three things: Justice, Truth and Peace." (Ethics of the Fathers 1:18.)

The memory of John Lennon will not soon fade. In truth, if his adulators settle down to serious estimation of his philosophy, the language of peace will become the official speech of our government and of our people and indeed the rule of peace will have a greater chance in a world shaken by the talk of war.

"May the Lord give strength unto our people. The Lord bless our people with peace."

JOHN LENNON: NO SECRET INTERIOR, JUST INTEGRITY

Robert Hilburn, Los Angeles Times, Los Angeles, CA, December 14, 1980

With the Beatles, John Lennon helped stretch rock 'n' roll from its infancy into an art form.

Yet it's Lennon the man whom I'll miss more than Lennon the rock 'n' roll star. That's not a shot at his music, but a tribute to the warmth of the man. Few people I've met in rock were as easy or as stimulating to be around.

The quality of his albums fell after the brilliant "Imagine" in 1971, but the former Beatle never lost the graciousness and enthusiasm that made him such a delightful host.

Perhaps the most comforting thought that can be passed on to fans saddened by his death is this: If you had been able to meet Lennon, you wouldn't have been disappointed. He was a person of profound commitment and integrity. In an age of tarnished heroes, he remained remarkably true to his ideals.

Beneath the hoopla over the Beatles and superstardom, Lennon was unusually unaffected. He was a man who could be equally thrilled by the simple pleasures of the rock 'n' roll music that he'd heard as a youth and by the promise of peace and love—not a Utopian fantasy for Lennon, but a legitimate if elusive social goal.

A LOT OF PEOPLE WERE CRYING

Al Carter, The Daily Oklahoman, Oklahoma City, OK,
December 11, 1980

Now we are 30, and after a childhood spent staring down bayonets and standing up to parental authority, it seems odd that the silent creak of the human odometer could leave us in such a funk.

Some of us are bald. Some of us have dropped the ultimate surprise and made babies (Look, Ma! No chromosome damage!) and despite all that sex education, we still can't figure out where they came from.

We've learned how to tie ties and make turkey stuffing. Some of us have secretaries. Some are women secretaries.

Knowing all that, it's a wonder that anyone on this planet would get upset over the death of a rock 'n roll star. But a lot of us had trouble weathering the news Monday night and throughout the day Tuesday. A lot of us cried.

A lot of us cried and asked those who we knew wouldn't cry to understand. But a lot of those people were crying, too.

All of which must say something about the life of John Lennon and the magical, mysterious, emotional tour that was the 1960s. To a generation that refused to believe in the impossibility of change, the Beatles are gone forever and that cannot be changed. The realization is overwhelmingly sad.

To a generation, the Beatles were as basic as air. The age of mass media dictated that life itself needed a musical score, and for one very crazy decade, Paul McCartney called the beat and John Lennon wrote the speeches.

The Beatles were the avenue down which a generation marched and matured, and for two reasons: The timing was perfect; and the talent was real.

John Kennedy's murder stunned people of every age. But its effect on teens and pre-teens was traumatic—a radiant president struck down in an incident missed by the all-powerful television set and at the hand of an unseen assassin whose identity is still questioned.

With the Beatles, no item was left undisclosed—not even the label on Ringo's undershorts. The Beatles were on television, at the movies, at the local coliseum. They were 68 cents plus tax at the record counter.

The world wanted "different," and the Beatles were different in every way, every day of your life. No one would harm a Beatle. Walter Cronkite would never have to announce that a Beatle had been shot dead. Until now.

Yet, there would have been no Beatle phenomenon—and less of a change in styles and attitudes—had Lennon and McCartney not been such gifted artists. Educators at mid-century spoke of the great poets and composers, but it did not escape the lunchsack set that Keats and Longfellow and Gilbert and Sullivan were long dead and had not been replaced.

So a generation drafted the Beatles, accepted society's tagging it "pop" instead of art and then mellowed with a sophisticated pride when its very own discovery made fans of Leonard Bernstein and Arthur Fiedler and later helped influence the thinking of every generation. Pretty heavy stuff for 12-year-olds to grow up on.

The Beatles were something close and personal in an ugly world. They were a point of reference for growing up: Wishing you had $5 to attend a concert, hearing Sgt. Pepper's for the first time, wondering if Paul was dead, finding out that John was.

To many this week, the feelings of despair and resignation rival the impact felt 17 years ago when childhood illusions were shattered by the news from Dallas. John Kennedy and Martin Luther King shaped the world through politics. John Lennon shaped it through music.

There is that familiar, haunting urge to do something when nothing can be done. That is why the record stores won't be able to keep Lennon records in stock for a while. That's why I felt Tuesday night might be a good time to buy a book of Beatles lyrics and why the guy at the cash register, every mother's son, was wearing a photo button of John Lennon.

"That's a good choice," he said.

"It's been a rough day," I said.

"Yeah," he said. "It has."

JOHN LENNON

George Melly, Punch, London, December 12, 1980

Reading the newspapers, listening to the radio and television, you get the impression that everybody loved and has always loved John Lennon. Well they didn't. They loved Ringo and respected George and were seduced by Paul, but after the original honeymoon period with "The Fab Four," they recognised, quite correctly, that John couldn't be bought, wouldn't compromise, tried to change the world through a series of gestures which, because they were seriously intended but expressed symbolically, were bound to fail and could be dismissed with contemptuous laughter. Only a week or two ago the news that he never went out but baked bread every day and looked after his son, seemed good enough for a few schnide paragraphs. Lennon, the rich hippy with his six apartments and that ugly Japanese wife. Lennon, the cock-flasher, acorn-sender, bed-in-freak. Lennon, the Howard Hughes of rock.

Well, Lennon had just begun to go out again, was making a new album, and had renewed his love affair with New York as a city, "the safest on earth," and then a psychopath who identified with him pulled a gun and shot him dead. "I just shot John Lennon," he told the janitor. "Ungrammatical," said my friend Derek Taylor with angry despair. He believes a contempt for language shows a contempt for life. Lennon respected language.

Difficult to remember, ploughing through the eulogies in every newspaper, that Lennon was for a long time trapped in an enormous cage called the United States. If he left, they told him, he wouldn't be allowed back, so despite a great deal of pressure he wouldn't leave, and anyway he knew and they knew it wasn't the marijuana bust as they pretended. It was his opposition to the war that had enraged the Nixon administration.

Lennon was always the awkward one. There was the tremendous fuss when he said that at that moment the Beatles were more famous than Jesus Christ, which was in a sense true. He didn't say better or holier or eternally more famous, just more famous *then;* a statement of fact for which they burnt his records.

And yet I wouldn't exactly accuse the media of hypocrisy. They do, and I'm writing this only two days after his death, feel outrage because they sense that he was someone who was part of a whole generation's youth, someone who changed the sensibility of almost everybody, who proved, together with a few other key figures, that poetry was not an esoteric art but available for all. A newspaper today printed the famous photograph of Yoko and him showing their bare bottoms. At the time the response was outrage or ridicule. Now they look only vulnerable, only human.

The boy who killed him wanted attention. "Happiness," the Beatles once sung with satirical phallic intentions, "is a warm gun." The boy took it literally. The boy is happy. He is, for a moment, as famous as his victim. What Tom Wolfe called "The Me Decade" has found its pathetic spokesman.

I met Lennon several times and sometimes we got on and sometimes we didn't. I was one of the trad generation and he hated that because he felt that initially the jazz men had treated him with contempt, blocked his way and that of the music he believed in. When his first book, *In His Own Write,* was published I reviewed it favourably but at the publisher's party we nearly came to blows because I insisted, and would still insist, that the Black origins from which his very early songs derived were superior. He seemed to me arrogant. I suspect, with some reason, that he found me patronising. He was a hard man then, not at all the "happy little rocker" of the publicity handouts.

I didn't meet him again until after the Beatles had broken up when he and Yoko were on the same chat show. They were very quiet and benign and we had a friendly if rather disoriented conversation of some length. With his long hair and granny glasses, his gentle and affectionate manner, it was hard to recognise the tight-mouthed aggressive young man of five years earlier. We parted with much of that bear-hugging which was the fashion of the time. I had just published a book which was critical of what I felt were their rather *déja vù* activities. I felt guilty about it. They seemed so at peace, and I thought Yoko was lovely.

Then they broke up and John had his hair cut and in the company of the singer, Harry Nilsson, that most seductive of ravers, hit the town again. They were known as "The Vampires" because they only came out at night. Rumours of shattered picture windows reached me. The old Lennon had surfaced with a vengeance.

I was in L.A. with Derek Taylor, formerly the Beatles P.R.O. and some time later a director of the ill-fated Apple. We were trying in vain to persuade Warner Brothers, for whom he was working, that there was a reason to invest some money in a middle-aged jazz-singer who had just gone back on the road. We were staying in a bungalow which was an annex of the Chateau Marmont, that grotesquely beautiful example of Spanish Hollywood kitsch. I got up one morning and came out of the bedroom to confront Derek and John returning, with steam coming out of their ears, from a night on the tiles. It was a little tentative to start with. This was no longer the loving hippy but the old aggressive scouser full of drink and God knows what else; the rocker who had made it facing the trad-singer who'd tried to block his way. However, there was something we shared in common. We were both Liverpudlians and Liverpool is the most chauvinist place in the world. "Liverpool," wrote Alun Owen, who also wrote *A Hard Day's Night,* "scars its children for life."

Somehow we got on to a scouse wrestler who spanned both our childhoods. His name was Jackie Pye and his specialty was throwing snot at the referee. With the palm trees of L.A. looming up through the smog outside, we recreated those nights in the smoky Liverpool stadium of twenty years before when Jackie Pye, to the delighted outrage of the crowd, performed his gimmick. It was an hysterical and unforgettable couple of hours.

He was less sympathetic in New York a few months later when I was singing there. Derek and I were staying in The Algonquin. Lennon and Nilsson showed up there "Baying for broken glass." John rang up my publicity agent at 2 a.m. and demanded carnal knowledge. She was not best pleased, and, perhaps to his surprise, made it clear.

His separation from Yoko didn't work out. They found they needed each other too much and the long rave-up was over. In their ever-growing complex of apartments Lennon became a recluse. He was only just ready to come out.

John Lennon offered an insoluble paradox. His huge fortune reduced the value of his gestures (he and Yoko once arrived in a white Rolls to fast on the steps of a church), and yet without his fame those same gestures would have passed unnoticed. He showed at all times great courage and indifference to mockery, but what he wanted—peace, goodwill, love—remain as elusive as ever. He was not ashamed to show that he had a penis and that he loved his wife, but his lasting value is in his music both before and after the Beatles broke up. Here he was both tough and tender, exact and universal, funny and tragic.

The sheer bulk of his obituaries is mysterious, beyond logic. Nothing he hoped for came about: wars rage, people hate, a young man buys a gun and waits outside the Dakota building; and yet everyone, it seems, feels diminished by his death.

JOHN LENNON

Chicago Tribune, Chicago, IL, December 10, 1980

For people of a certain age, born to the new world of the Bomb and the baby boom, nurtured in the optimistic years following the Korean War, and coming into adulthood in the dark days of Viet Nam, the death of John Lennon sets off a series of aftershocks: Irony that the violence his songs condemned felled him at last on the cold streets of New York. Sadness that having survived the worst of the dark days—survived all the foolish enthusiasms as well as the tragic historical forces that swept over that period—he should have been killed in such an absurd and apparently gratuitous way. And ultimately, the grief that comes when a part of our own lives dies.

The music of the Beatles was in a way the embodiment of all the wrenching changes that confronted a generation coming of age. It was cute when we were cute and innocent. The Beatles wanted us to hold hands, wanted Beethoven to roll over, wanted to dance. The rebellion in their longish hair when they first appeared in the United States seems so quaint today. The times grew worse, and rebellion more real. The music pleaded for peace. It experimented with drugs and other faddish salvations. And toward the end it grew bitter. Happiness was a warm gun.

It is difficult now to hear John Lennon's music of his Beatles days without having all those conflicted memories—of enjoying and suffering them. And it is also difficult to forget how much Mr. Lennon and his colleagues enriched popular music.

The shock at Mr. Lennon's death is more than simply the reaction of a group of dedicated, undaunted fans. Even those who may not have thought about him much in recent years except on quiet evenings when they dusted off the old Sgt. Pepper album and put it on the machine just for old time's sake—even they will grieve.

Like all of us, John Lennon grew older and perhaps a little wiser. And he often said, when asked whether the Beatles would ever come together again, that he did not like to look back. But when he was gunned down, some small, sustaining part of our youth—a part filled in equal measures with joy and folly and pain—died, too.

JOHN ONO LENNON: 1940-1980

Steve Acker, Capital Reporter, Jackson, MS, December 11, 1980

The re-union the world has waited ten years for is now about to be. The head, the hands, and the feet of the Beatles are to be joined together again. Tragically, it is to mourn the death of the soul that gave them life.

For nearly 17 years John Lennon was the living personification of our society. As a Beatle he shared in the creation of the greatest popular music the world has ever heard.

Because of his genius, the Beatles became more than a very good band. They became the spokesmen for a generation about to face Vietnam, racial war, and loss of belief in the goodness of its leaders.

Just as the first postwar generation defiantly survived growing up in the bitterness of the Sixties and the bewilderment of the Seventies to re-discover the eternal values of love, home, and family; so, too, did John Lennon.

He had recently emerged from five years of "baking bread and looking after the baby" with a new record and a fresh enthusiasm for talking with the press. His new message, like his earlier ones, mirrored the lives of an entire generation.

He and the wife he loved with incredible passion, Yoko Ono, seemed to be saying to us, "Let's still give peace a chance, but let's find it at home first. That's what it's really all about." He always said, "don't follow leaders," and, contrary to the belief of those who never understood, no one even followed John Lennon.

He just happened to be going the same way we were.

Bob Batz, Jr., Dayton Daily News, Dayton, OH, December 10, 1980

When Lennon died, I lost a friend I've never met, a friend I've never talked to, a friend I've never seen in person, but a friend, nevertheless.

JOHN LENNON'S DEATH

Columbus Citizen-Journal, Columbus, OH, December 11, 1980

You did not have to be a member of the Beatles generation to know that a revolution in popular music, personal attitudes and life styles was in the making in the mid-1960s. And the Beatles symbolized that revolution more than any other rock group did.

John Lennon probably was the most creative of the Beatles. He certainly was the most intellectual and the most ideological.

We are shocked, saddened and angered at the murder of this peaceable, gentle man.

"Any man's death diminishes me," John Donne wrote more than 300 years ago. As the outpouring of sentiment over Lennon around the world testifies, some deaths diminish more than others. Millions feel his death keenly and personally.

Lennon's place in the history of rock music is secure. At the time of his death, he was only 40 and had just launched a comeback with a new album, his first in six years. We will never know what unwritten songs perished with him.

THE SURREAL GENIUS OF ROCK

Ray Connolly, Liverpool Daily Post, England, December 10, 1980

At 3:30 on Monday afternoon my telephone rang. It was Yoko Ono calling from New York.

"Okay, when are you coming over to do this interview with John and me?" she said.

"Great, the sooner the better," she answered. And at 5:30 this morning I learned that I was too late.

John Lennon was the Beatle who dazzled. He was the most literate of all the rock writers.

He took rock into the world of surrealism: he invented the Walrus, the Glass Onion, Lucy in the Sky with Diamonds and the Nowhere Man.

As a child, he had been much impressed by the stories of Lewis Carroll. As a man, he became the dream weaver for my generation.

To most people there were four Beatles, but to some of us there were really only two who mattered.

As John told me time and time again: "Paul and I are the Beatles. We write the songs."

Perhaps he was being less than appreciative of the contributions made by George Harrison and Ringo Starr, but his directness was hard to dispute.

The Beatles were that magical synthesis of sound which resulted from the melodic brilliance of McCartney and the wit and barbed sarcasm of John Lennon. Together, they complemented each other like no other two composers in this century.

During the early years of their careers, following their famous meeting as schoolboys at a church fete, they rode in tandem, one offering a couple of lines and chord structure, and then the other taking over.

But as their careers rocketed in the mid-1960's they began to write more and more separately and their two very different styles became increasingly marked. Although John liked to think of himself as a hard, tough rocker, he was actually extremely sensitive and artistic, and his songs showed this.

He wrote many beautiful melodies but his real joy was playing with words, articulating the loneliness which always seemed to surround him.

His childhood was sad. He was deserted by his father and brought up by an aunt after his mother had been killed in a road accident, and although he tried to reflect a tough exterior, and could be extremely cruel on occasions, there was always a naked streak of vulnerability about him.

In the early 1960's, when Brian Epstein finally achieved recognition for the Beatles, it was John who took on the mantle of leader, mainly because he was older than Paul.

The speed of events in the 1960's played havoc with his nerves, and he went quickly from drink to pills and then heavier drugs.

But despite all the hysteria and all the lunacy surrounding him during those times, the music and images poured out of him in a bewildering display, bare-faced autobiographical testiments to his own unhappiness, like Help! and In My Life, and disturbing LSD-influenced pieces such as A Day in the Life and Strawberry Fields Forever.

John Lennon could detect the mood of the time better than anyone I have ever known. When he sang All You Need Is Love he produced an anthem for the flower generation. When he wrote Give Peace A Chance, he gave us a song which has become part of every protest movement in the Western world.

While Paul McCartney was always the more conservative of the two, John rushed head long into everything which seemed new and exciting.

With a university education he might have been a different person. I always suspected that he was a frustrated intellectual who attracted to himself the flotsam and jetsam of 1960's characters, who could impress him with their seeming unconventionality.

He was easily flattered by charlatans, but always grateful for favours.

During the late 1960's and early 1970's he was a very kind and generous friend to me. But as the decade passed our contracts became fewer, just the odd postcard now and again as he went further into his reclusive shell.

Then recently he produced his first new album in seven years. He was 40, and had spent enough time "babysitting" with his five-year-old son, Sean. He wanted to get out and about again. He was, in the words of his current hit record Starting Over.

I was to have spent this afternoon and this evening with John Lennon in New York.

I am privileged to have known him.

WE'VE LOST PART OF OURSELVES

Nigel Willmott, Tribune, London, December 19, 1980

What we have now lost is a part of ourselves. He helped create our world—brought it into consciousness with his images, phrases, words, refrains. The sting in the tail is that the optimism of our world in those days was misplaced. The irreversible shift in power and wealth that we thought would happen, if we bought enough Beatles LPs, never happened. The tuneful revolt of the plebs was soon the latest style available down the Kings Road and all high street shops from Friday.

Lennon came to his politics fitfully and idiosyncratically because it was implicit in his music, and he stuck to it in his way to the end—despite the preference of the media to ignore, ridicule or gloss over them. He realised culture and politics are intrinsically bound up with each other. You can't just fill the world with silly love songs.

What's wrong with that is that the power of artistic creation comes from its roots in social reality. And you can't, like too many on the Left seem to feel, just smear a bit of appetising culture on to the industrial struggle, like jam. People's consciousness of the world is created by their culture, and politics can only reveal what is already there—bring it out, give it definition, like a brass rubbing.

Beatles culture was irreverent, confident, optimistic, subversive. Four healthy, good looking, welfare-state, working-class lads on stage, open, upright, belting out joyful songs. But this gang of four lost their cultural struggle, too. The seminal image of the late seventies, the sickly, hunched, disdainful figure of Johnny Rotten, surly Lennon's spiritual heir, tells all.

In the end, the new world that was to be could only be imagined, as it was, beautifully, poetically, wistfully in Lennon's best song as a solo artist:

> *imagine no possessions*
> *I wonder if you can*
> *no need for greed or hunger*
> *a brotherhood of man*
> *imagine all the people*
> *sharing all the world . . .*

Billboard, Los Angeles, CA, December 20, 1980

Atlantic's John Belushi says: "John was my idol. As an individual and an artist he was supreme. He and the Beatles helped to reshape our musical heritage, our feelings about life and the way we looked at everything. Since the emergence of John and the Beatles, nothing has been the same for us. It's impossible to imagine the world without him."

LOST: ANOTHER GREAT SPIRIT

*Robert L. Huntington, Jr. to The Hartford Courant, Hartford, CT,
December 16, 1980*

The ironies of John Lennon's death are many. We are
reminded of the facts that he had waged a long, painful,
expensive legal battle for the right to live in this country, that he
had made every effort to avoid the public limelight in recent
years, that no popular musician has devoted more creative
energy to expressing the power of mature love, that he and his
wife were just beginning a positive, happy new phase of their
artistic careers, and that he had gladly autographed an album
for the man who later shot him. But ironies are not the heart of
the matter here.

In John Lennon's passing, the world has lost another free
man, another great spirit. We've lost the powerful example of a
man who was not afraid to call life as he saw it, not afraid to face
the consequence of his actions, and not afraid to move beyond
others' expectations of him. More than any of the other Beatles,
Lennon seemed to symbolize the spiritual quest that so many
in the '60s generation have gone through. A casual glance
through some old Beatle album covers will show even the most
disinterested onlooker and Lennon was a man constantly in
change, never content to rest on past successes.

Whenever we thought we had him figured out, he was
moving on—comparing the early Beatles' popularity to that of
Jesus, sitting at the feet of the Maharishi Mahesh Yogi, marrying
an older Oriental woman whose art and music we've never
been able to get used to, taking a stand against the Vietnam war,
staging a week-long sleep-in for peace, fighting the U.S.
government in court, trading the glamour of superstardom for
the quiet anonymity of New York City apartment life.

In an age when heroes are on the endangered species list,
John Lennon will be sorely missed. His wit, courage, and
positive affirmation of life and love were of a strength sufficient

to give hope and determination to millions of other less adventurous souls. Lennon himself realized the power of example that he wielded over all those who knew him through his lyrics. In his caustic warning entitled "God," Lennon pleaded with us not to put our faith in heroes, doctrines, and movements. His message was simple but elusive: "Believe in yourself."

JOHN LENNON'S MUSIC WILL NEVER DIE

John Murray to The Denver Post, Denver, CO, December 15, 1980

His is a great and singular loss. When such a person dies we are all diminished. The brutal circumstances of this life's end make his loss seem all the more horrible.

John Lennon was a gifted poet and musician. Only a very few of those prominent in popular music have been both. Still fewer have achieved his level of understanding and his sensitive, sympathetic view of life, particularly of its pathos.

Lennon wrote of human suffering, alienation, loneliness and despair. He also wrote of love, hope, compassion and forgiveness. His favorite theme, one that can be found in his earliest and in his last songs, was that of reconciliation.

In his late 20s he became passionately committed to various social causes, such as ending the Vietnam War, feminism and the plight of the worker. None had as much meaning for his as the cause of world peace, a cause which is especially relevant in the world today.

Twenty-five centuries ago, in Athens, there was a popular and prolific songwriter named Pindar. All that remains of his life work, though, are a few scattered lyrics. The music itself is gone forever. The only bright aspect in today's black tragedy is that John Lennon, unlike Pindar and others, will never die. He left the best part of himself in his songs, and, because of the breakthroughs in recording and transcribing, people 2,500 years from now will be able to marvel at, to sing and dance to his wonderful creations.

What they will wonder, and what we will wonder, too, is what he might have gone on to write had he lived. He was a young man, only 40. He had just emerged from five years of self-imposed exile, a period of intense self-examination and development, and his latest album promised new beginnings. They, and we, will never know what lovely melodies and immortal lyrics died with him. But in the end they will love him, as we did, as a human being giving the fullest and finest expression of himself, sharing his life and his genius because he loved us all. He made us hear the music and see the hope amid the harsh cacophony and shocking horror of this world.

Billboard, Los Angeles, CA, December 20, 1980

From Australia, Graham Russell of Air Supply: "John was one of the handful of true rock poets and his lyrics always bore the stamp of his unique mind. Listening to them now they seem unbearably poignant, full of other shades of meanings now that he has gone."

THE PROMISE IS GONE...

Ellen Goodman, The Boston Globe, Boston, MA, December 13, 1980

I had seen his face only last Sunday: he and the other three looking out from 1960s buttons and posters. The four were all encased in glass, like cameos of Queen Victoria. They were captured in a Beatles booth at an antique show.

It startled me then to see the Beatles sold as something old. But it is always surprising when our youth becomes a collector's item.

On Tuesday, I saw his face again, on the front page. John Lennon, the most complex of the Beatles, had been shot dead by a loony, a cuckoo, a nutcake—the New York police used all the familiar words, including "allegedly." The killer apparently was some crazed cousin to all the crackpots and criminals who can buy guns as easily as Christmas trees. Amen to that.

But the Lennon I'll miss isn't the brilliant Beatle of the '60s with his hair "rebelliously" grown below his ears. That John Lennon exists on my records. The man I'll miss is the one I just met again, the man of the '80s, moving in new ways, making new sounds. Five bullets wiped out this father, husband, musician...human work in progress.

I am more a member of the Beatles generation than the fans' generation. So I was moved by the emergence of John Lennon at 40.

It was good to see him selling Promise at Forty. Not depressions, not complacency, not mania, but Promise. "It's quite possible," he said, "to do anything."

The new record he made with his wife, Yoko Ono, "Double Fantasy," was the work of a survivor. "You have to give thanks to God or whatever is up there [for] the fact that we all survived—survived Vietnam or Watergate, the tremendous upheaval of the whole world," he said in an ironic prelude to his death.

But it wasn't just the decades he'd survived. He'd overcome something else: other people's expectations.

John Lennon got lost for a time, wandering in the body of The Famous John Lennon. He became so public a person that his life became a role he was playing. Other people were the directors.

There were the fans who expected him to be a Beatle Forever, until he ended up singing "I Wanna Hold Your Hand" in Las Vegas nightclubs. There were the business managers who wanted him to be their product. "I was a machine," he said, "that was supposed to produce so much creative something and give it out periodically for approval to justify my existence on earth."

There were even people who expected him to self-destruct like Dylan Thomas or the rock stars with needle tracks up their arms. "I'd just naively accepted the idea," he said, "that an artist had to self-destruct in order to create."

He survived all these expectations by getting better, saner, older. In 1975, he jumped into his private life as if it were a lifeboat. His fans called it seclusion. He called it becoming a "househusband." But he got in touch with the routines that root all of us, with daily-ness. He took care of his child, instead of being taken care of like a child. He let himself go into his new rhythms.

Five years later, this fall, he and his wife came out with music and words. He talked about men and women "Starting Over," about balancing family and work, about growing up.

"Is it possible to have a life centered around a family and a child and still be an artist?" he asked one reporter. "When I look at the relative importance of what life is about, I can't quite convince myself that making a record or having a career is more important or even as important as my child, or any child," he told another.

The man changed, and typically refused to apologize or simplify it. "The attitude is that when you change when you get older there's something wrong with that. Whatever changes I'm going through because I'm 40 I'm thankful for, because they give me some insight into the madness I've been living all myself."

In a way he was talking to and for his own generation. "I'm saying, 'Here I am now, how are you? How's your relationship going? Did you get through it all? Wasn't the '70s a drag, you know? Well, here we are, let's make the '80s great because it's up to us to make what we can of it.' "

John Lennon of the '60s survived so much—even pessimism—only to get murdered. He made a life late and died early.

Did his murderer aim for the '60s superstar, the Beatle, the face under glass? What craziness and waste. You can't kill what a man has already done. You can only kill what might have come next.

The antique John Lennon had already been preserved. Dammit, it's the promise that's gone.

LENNON ON RECORD: TWO DECADES OF POP GENIUS

Bill Ashton, The Miami Herald, Miami, FL, December 14, 1980

John Lennon didn't think a great deal of his abilities as a musician. He once said in an interview, "I play the piano even worse than I play guitar." But Lennon knew he could write strong songs and produce great records.

The millions who agreed with him bought his records and listened to his lyrics, sometimes looking for hidden meanings or words to live by. His music made people happy, it made people angry, it made people think and it made them wonder. The people who heard something of themselves in the music made Lennon a rich and famous man.

THE LAST DAY IN THE LIFE

Jay Cocks, Time, December 22, 1980

The outpouring of grief, wonder and shared devastation that followed Lennon's death had the same breadth and intensity as the reaction to the killing of a world figure: some bold and popular politician, like John or Robert Kennedy, or a spiritual leader, like Martin Luther King Jr. But Lennon was a creature of poetic political metaphor, and his spiritual consciousness was directed inward, as a way of nurturing and widening his creative force. That was what made the impact, and the difference—the shock of his imagination, the penetrating and pervasive traces of his genius—and it was the loss of all that, in so abrupt and awful a way, that was mourned last week, all over the world. The last *Day in the Life,* "I read the news today oh boy..."

Lennon's death was not like Elvis Presley's. Presley seemed, at the end, trapped, defeated and hopeless. Lennon could have gone that way too, could have destroyed himself. But he did something harder. He lived. And, for all the fame and finance, that seemed to be what he took the most pride in.

"He beat the rock-'n'-roll life," Steve Van Zandt said the day after Lennon died. "Beat the drugs, beat the fame, beat the damage. He was the only guy who beat it all." That was the victory Mark Chapman took from John Lennon; who had an abundance of what everyone wants and wanted only what so many others have, and take for granted. A home and family. Some still center of love. A life. One minute more.

LENNON WITHOUT TEARS

Andrew Kopkind, The Soho News, New York, NY,
December 17, 1980

John Lennon's global sendoff Sunday was more a corona-
tion than a funeral, an act of elevation rather than a last
goodbye. In a way that was unpredicted and unpredictable,
"our Beatle" is now our king, the immortal incarnation of the
spirit of the '60s, the defining figurehead of a formless
generation. In the parks and public squares from Liverpool to
L.A. the multitudes mourned, but that show of grief was also an
act of homage—to the single songsmith, saint and symbol who
now sums up everything we are.

Mere mortal monarchs express the essence of their
bounded realms. In their years on the throne (or, in the case of
democratic royalty, in their terms in office) they serve to unify
their subjects by the ritual affirmation of the national char
acter—that special Englishness, Dutchness, Frenchness. But
death can confer a curious immortality and an unbounded
domain on heroes. "Lennon Lives"—a conspicuous slogan
scrawled on signboards in Central Park—rings true: the
posthumous president (he might prefer the democratic form)
of Woodstock Nation will permanently define the specialness
of a generation that transcends frontiers, class and ideology.
Young insurgent workers in Gdansk, lawyers in Atlanta, nurses
in New York; supermarket stockmen, computer programmers,
wheeler-dealers, stars and layabouts who came of age in the
Beatle years have finally found a focus in John Lennon.

The appointment of a spiritual leader presents a crisis in
personal identity as well as social history, and Sunday's
ceremony contained both of those elements. The cab driver
who drove us home from the park had been listening to a live
broadcast of the event on the radio, but he was curious about
the "feeling" in the park. "Will you remember it for the rest of
your life?" he asked.

I was momentarily startled by the gravity of his question, but I hardly hesitated to answer yes. It had the "feeling" of Woodstock, of the 1969 antiwar mobilization in Washington: those massive gatherings that served as identity checks as well as historical blips. People in the park last Sunday stared intensely at each other, as they might study themselves in a mirror. What they saw, at the very least, was the persistence of their past.

There have been crowded concerts and sectarian rallies in the last decade, but none of them have had the inclusive, definitive character of the great gatherings of the '60s—until the Lennon memorial. Once more, 10 years after, we recognized the specialness of our "nationhood," appraised—and maybe mourned—our history. Everything was the same—and different.

My friend Roger, a lawyer in his early 30s, told me that he wandered through the throng alone, trying to detect the collective sensibility he knew "in the old days." But although the people *looked* right, they emanated isolation instead of community. "There was nothing to connect us," he said sadly, "except the memory of how we once were connected."

Lennon knew all about isolation; he wrote a song about it nine years ago. Indeed, his creative genius and his historical importance consist in large measure in an unerring sense of prophecy and timing. Fans be damned; he broke up the Beatles at the moment he saw that the group had lost its dynamic of artistic development. His politics were sincere but safe: give peace a chance rather than struggle and trash. "The war is over," he exclaimed, but the wish did not make the fact. "All you need is love" was comforting but inadequate. Soon he recoiled at the increasingly revolutionary adventures of the militants and proclaimed that he didn't want a revolution at all; in fact, he counseled his fans to simply "let it be."

As the counter-culture drifted into drugs, mysticism and exotic psychotherapies, Lennon led the parade, acid-tripping, Maharishi-grouping and primal screaming. Long before Tom

Wolfe, Lennon announced the advent of the Me Generation, declaring his disbelief in every cause, cult hero and movement—the Kennedys, Jesus, Gita, Zimmerman, the Beatles: "I just believe in me; Yoko and me."

Once a working-class hero, he now was a captain of the *haute bourgeoisie,* multiplying his fortune by dealing in ranching, real estate and other diversified enterprises. Like the rest of the Beatles generation, his work and life were becoming private rather than communal. Even his good deeds were personal: for charity, he gave turkeys and woolen scarves to the needy in his West Side neighborhood. At last, he idealized the nuclear family ideal with a pluperfect marriage, a quiet life in the Dakota and a new record of unrelenting sentimentality. He could be inducted into the Moral Majority. No wonder he succeeded; more than any other performer of his era, he was a "crossover" phenomenon, adulated by the mass media and the alternative culture. He no longer posed a threat to the arbiters of good manners and the protectors of public order. Quite the other way: here was a living lesson of how an unruly, undisciplined youth of the lower class could acquire good manners and morals, not to mention an estate of $235 million.

Lennon's life is replete with contradictions—as are the lives of those for whom he is now a spiritual avatar. The generational character he defines is informed by the same dreams and delusions, the confrontations and evasions that Lennon experienced. There is no way, of course, to avoid the contradictions—to defeat isolation, pretend that money is unimportant, forget charity, deprive oneself of loving intimacy. They are facts of a larger social reality that rock musicians can never revive. The best anyone can do in the face of history is to act with as much inner honesty and authenticity as possible— and that, above all, is how Lennon achieved his heroic stature.

A week ago no one would have imagined the immense impact of John Lennon's death. If a list had been drawn of potential cult heroes of the '60s, his name might well have been included, but in fact he had slipped out of the limelight for so long that his social significance was drastically diminished. Only in death did his real role become clear. Who else is there? No political activist, no movie star, no other performer comes close: Dylan is too bitter and guilt-ridden, Jagger suffers from retarded adolescence, the other Beatles are ordinary people, Tom Hayden is abrasive, Abbie Hoffman is a goof, Jane Fonda is too shallow.

Lennon had honesty, authenticity, courage, depth, warmth and vision—the best qualities of the '60s generation. He projected a dream of utopia where peace, love and community reigned unchallenged by meanies. Cynics may scorn, but that utopian vision is what gave the people of the '60s a measure of meaning to their lives that they remember well but may never see again.

Even the remembrance of utopia gives that generation a unique coherence as it travels through the decades—the rat moving through the body of a python, intact and isolated from everything before and behind it, still self-conscious and undigested. Imagination of perfection does not create utopia but it offers hope that can make action and living worthwhile. Its opposite—despair—is all too prevalent in this day and age, and it leads nowhere. John Lennon never was a nowhere man.

Billboard, Los Angeles, CA, December 20, 1980

Says Smokey Robinson: "Forty is an early age to have to leave this planet—but as a performer, the way Lennon was killed is very frightening and tragic to me. He was truly one of the world's greatest musical innovators and I'm sure he will be missed and mourned by many, especially those of us who are his peers."

JOHN LENNON'S DREAM IS OVER

'Our Voice,' The Evening Bulletin, Philadelphia, PA, December 10, 1980

John Lennon's death diminishes the lives of more than those of us in his generation. He and the Beatles created a revolution in popular music and became the symbols of a generation in ferment.

Lennon was struck down in a senseless act of violence Monday night that was the antithesis of his philosophy of love, peace, harmony, the sense of oneness he dreamed of for all of us in his Yellow Submarine.

John Lennon was a musician, a composer, a bearer of messages, the "thinking man's Beatle."

In 1964 he burst onto the American scene as a member of the Beatles. The frenzy the moptops from Liverpool created was considered just a fleeting infatuation. What developed was a love affair and a social awakening that sank into the consciences of millions.

No popular musical group has had the impact of the Beatles, a name made up by Lennon himself as a parody on "beat" as in the "beat generation" and an earlier rock-and-roll group, Buddy Holly and the Crickets. Their early songs crooned love stories, but by the mid-'60s they rocked the rock movement. They proved music could be more than notes, that it could be noteworthy. It no longer mattered whether it had a beat. It now carried a message. The Beatles wrote the themes for a generation of change. They tried to explain that generation and the revolution in attitudes it created.

The focus of the '60s and '70s was of counterculture, of anti-heroes, of drugs, of challenge to authority and resistance to war. Lennon's music reflected those struggles.

A generation fed on the Beatles' music and messages must now live with the meaninglessness of his death. As reflected in the title of one song, "The Dream Is Over."

Recently, Lennon and his wife, Yoko Ono, came out of a seclusion to cut an album, "Double Fantasy." In Lennon's words, it was conceived as a "dialogue on love." The generation that was nurtured on his music must now continue this dialogue without him.

DREAM IS ENDED

Savannah Morning News, Savannah, GA, December 11, 1980

Not all of us understood or appreciated John Lennon, or even the other Beatles with whom he gained fame. But many did, particularly those of the younger generations who grew up dancing, listening to and—most important—enjoying the Beatles' music. They are the ones who are saddened.

Lennon was the most outspoken, controversial and politically aware of the quartet of musicians Ed Sullivan invited to this country from England to be on his show in 1964, a performance that would prove a cataclysmic event. Many disdained his politics, many more his life style.

But agree with him or not, like him or not—Lennon contributed heavily to a revolution of modern music. The Beatles' performing style, their beat, even their dress and hairdos, were originals of which there have been many copies. They, like Elvis Presley, became giant prototypes in their field.

Lennon moved from liberalism nearly to a form of conservatism in the last few years, concentrating attention on home and family, and he became a philosopher of a sort. His recently expressed philosophical views bear repeating here because they are beamed at those who may hold doubts and fears about the future. He referred to the "fear of the unknown," and said:

"To be frightened of what (the unknown) is sends everybody scurrying around chasing dreams, illusions, wars, peace, love, hate, all that. Unknown is what it is. Accept that it's unknown and it's plain sailing...you're ahead of the game."

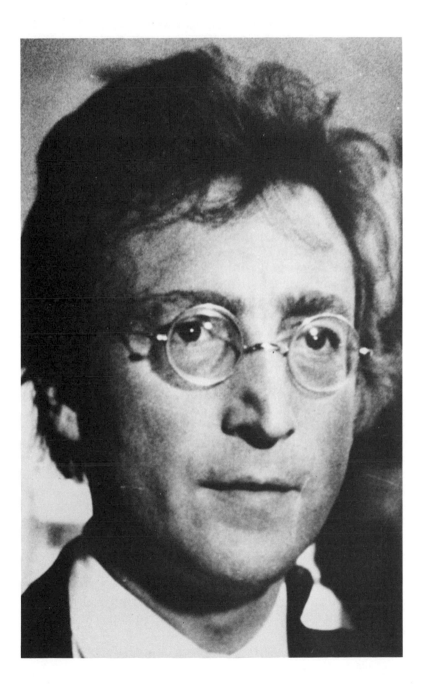

THE WALRUS WAS JOHN

Art Aguilar, East L.A. Tribune, Los Angeles, CA, December 17, 1980

There's a problem inherent to writing for a weekly newspaper. Deadlines sometimes come at the worst times and events you feel compelled to write about are often more than a week old before your commentary reaches print.

Yet, I think time stood still for a while last week when John Lennon died. Millions upon millions of words have been written about the man—there's little new I can add. Yet, I feel compelled to write something for my own sake if nothing else.

Lennon and the Beatles were my generation. I became a teen-ager at the same time the Beatles were born. We grew up together, went through changes together, became adults together.

I went to the Bowl and Dodger Stadium. Saw the closed-circuit Washington, D.C. concert at the Garmar. Marveled at this new form of rock-and-roll.

And, now I suffer with them—the remaining Beatles, Yoko, my generation, the world.

John Lennon was a great musician. When he developed a social conscience, he became a great man. But, above all (and in his own words) he was "a human being, mate."

Lennon suffered through the adulation that made him a powerful and rich man. His triumph and greatness came in the fact that he used his prominence for the good of the world, not just for the benefit of his ego.

Could you do that? Would you have the guts to turn away from the world as Lennon did in recent years to quietly straighten out your own life and use your resources for the good of others? (Many a charity and a cause were aided by the Lennons during their so-called quiet period.)

Would you have the guts to suddenly come back to the outside world and people who have forgotten you, many of whom do not even know you, as Lennon did just this past month?

It took an inner peace and an inner strength to accomplish this—it took a human being.

Many people have theories as to why the Beatles were so successful. Maybe their questions have now been answered.

Their music exuded humanity. These were real people, not golden idols. They sang of love and peace, hate and violence and the real differences between those subjects. They mirrored an ever-changing society and had guts enough to tell the people when they were going the wrong way.

And, when their usefulness was ended, they quit. No swan songs, no fanfare—they just quit. They showed us the way, but it was our world to build.

And build we did. Yet, we never forgot those who helped give us the tools. This is why John Lennon, ever so much the realist in life and in his music, will become a legend in death.

He was no prophet, no saint. At times people honestly hated the man (do we now forget his "more popular than Jesus" statement that, although true, caused widespread record-burnings and protest?). We knew he and his mates were, deep-down, just one of us.

What we owed him was our voice. Without the music of the Beatles we wouldn't have had the voice and the courage that brought down a government, ended a war and brought a new era of social conscience to America and the world.

When John Kennedy died, didn't the Beatles soothe our aching hearts with songs of teen-age love and the simple pleasures of life ("I Wanna Hold Your Hand," "Love Me Do," "She Loves You"). Simple, pleasant music during trying times, just what we needed.

But, when we got out of hand, we learned to look at ourselves and our faults in the "White Album." The song, "Revolution" is a marvel. It taunts both sides for taking themselves too seriously, but admits it's all necessary.

Lennon had the uncanny ability to look beneath the surface of the people and their problems and transform what he saw into words. He laughed at himself and others. He castigated himself as much as he did others.

But, he never overestimated his life and he never made himself bigger than he should have. At the end, he was as humble as he was in the beginning—maybe even more so.
Feel grief over his death—I do. Lennon and the Beatles were a great influence in my life.
I mourn the death of a man—a human being—one of us.
"A Day in the Life" seems so prophetic now—the news is rather sad.
The saddest news?
The walrus was John.

STRAWBERRY FIELDS FOREVER

Worcester Telegram, Worcester, MA, December 10, 1980

Standing at the torn edge that separates the generations, it is virtually impossible to know where to begin.
Does one start with the British invasion of the United States in 1964? Or with the rumors of Paul McCartney's death, with the long creative development that was the Beatles or with their breakup as a musical group.
Or does one start with the death of John Lennon? Does one work back, through the years that shaped so many lives in this and other countries? Through years when music became a force that tied so many people together? Those were years when John Lennon, songwriter, wrote the words to a generation's music.
John Lennon—radical, eccentric, poet and musician.
John Lennon and Paul McCartney, Ringo Starr and George Harrison. Those names and that music evoke rage in some about a lost generation, one that turned its back on standard values. They invoke a vision of a generation bewildered by Vietnam, by affluence—lost in a cloud of marijuana smoke.
Indeed, the Beatles, riding on Lennon's lyrics, seemed to many a menace that threatened to rip society apart.

Those who listened to the words, those searching for some other approach to life, were influenced by Lennon. Many did tune in, turn on and drop out, some for good, while their parents watched, horrified.

Through that decade the Beatles were shaping their music and shaping new ways of looking at life.

John Lennon shares the credit, or the blame, for Woodstock, long hair, the anti-war movement and a litany of alternatives that have come out of his music.

The music stands. It was not only a means of communicating, a way of bringing people together. It stands as a creative achievement unrivalled in its scope in this century. The haunting melodies of "While My Guitar Gently Weeps," the creative genius of "Sgt. Pepper's Lonely Hearts Club Band," "Norwegian Wood," remain. The satire of "Back in the U.S.S.R." and the musical experimentation of the White Album stand out.

Grief and memories—both fond and bitter—well up in the commotion over John Lennon's death.

Somehow the Beatles came to symbolize the pain and the joy of a whole decade of change, a time when people were reaching out to each other and were exploring new choices. Their impact is permanent.

The voice of a major observer and commentator on 20th century life—sometimes biting, sometimes loving, sometimes cynical, often criticized—has been stilled.

The argument will go on over whether Lennon—or McCartney—stand as individual creative giants. Neither reached the heights after the end of the Beatles that they reached as a group.

After a five-year interlude, John Lennon had started again. He had cut another record with a song called "Starting Over." That is finished.

There comes a day in everyone's life when death reaches out. Whether that death comes appropriately, or as did John Lennon's, in a senseless and brutal moment of tragedy—as the Lennon lyric has it, "life goes on, la."

The Talk of the Town, The New Yorker, December 15, 1980

Many complicated explanations have been given and will continue to be given for the depth of the grief that people all over the world have felt at the death of John Lennon, but one explanation may be quite simple. Beyond Lennon's great gifts as a composer, poet, and performer, beyond, and in spite of, his unparalleled and burdensome celebrity, he remained truly a man of the spirit—this humorous and friendly man who held on to his humanity against awesome odds, and who did not lecture us but, rather, spoke to us quietly, and in ways that we all understood. In what he said directly, in what he said in his very beautiful songs, and in the way he tried to live his far too brief life, the message that came through—and how rarely we hear such a message—was: Be peaceful, be loving, be gentle.

STARTING OVER: LIFE WITHOUT JOHN LENNON

Fay S. Joyce, St. Petersburg Times, St. Petersburg, FL, December 21, 1980

The story screamed from a thousand front pages. It took up at least the first 15 minutes of the CBS Evening News. A man and a teen-ager committed suicide. Thousands gathered at quickly-called vigils to shelter flickering candles against the wind, to cry and to hear the music again.

Until 10:50 p.m. on that irrevocable Monday night, did anyone know how much John Lennon meant to us?

We were shocked and depressed by the sudden brutality, the senseless assassination of a gentle soul, yes. But more than that, we understood in the awful instant of his death that John Lennon had not only created an extraordinary range of music, but also shaped a generation and its values.

We cried for John Lennon, and we cried because we knew those values of peace and love are slipping from our sight, growing as cold and small as bullets.

In 1964 the Beatles landed in America and reached into *us*, the scrawny, pimply teens who suddenly found we counted for something.

In the next few years, we would learn how much. Music was the language of our culture, of the baby boomers who created "the generation gap" and then leaped across it to carve a whole new world of styles, of attitudes, of thinking and relating.

When Lennon sang of the world being one, thousands of young adults had already experienced what he meant. It was easier to bum around Europe and make instant friends with foreigners who listened to the Beatles, wore blue jeans and long hair, were vaguely into Eastern religion and astrology and ate brown rice than it was to go home to Mom and Dad and their uptight, middle-class values in the suburbs.

The energy of the '60s exploded in a hundred directions: art, religion, writing, teaching, music, sex, drugs.

Suddenly the older generation gave in and began imitating. Men popped into pink shirts. Women discovered consciousness-raising groups. Sexual experimentation prospered, as did divorce lawyers.

In the full flower of our strength and headiness, we rebelled. Against the administration. Against racism. Against materialism. Against the cold world's lack of love. Against the rules. Against the war. Against everything we thought inhibited people and made them smaller.

Lennon and his wife Yoko Ono staged a simple protest during the Vietnam War. They stayed in bed for a week in

Amsterdam, and invited the newspaper photographers in. "The worst that can happen is we create a laugh," said Lennon. "But the best is the vibrations for peace get through."

Something got through. The war ended. The '60s ended. Bobby Kennedy and Martin Luther King ended. The Beatles broke up. Richard Nixon came and went. Overseas, the peace movement gave way to terrorists.

A few days before John Lennon was killed, I sat in a friend's apartment sipping a Lowenbrau. We discussed her plans to move into the $80,000 condominium she and her friend just bought in the suburbs.

"I used to be in peace marches," she said. "What happened to me?"

John Lennon answered that question by turning to his family, to traditional values of home and hearth that we had once found so boring. He stayed married. He raised a child. He kept house. He accepted the money his record royalties brought in. He wrote a song called *Starting Over.*

As for the rest of us, we didn't change the world. Most of us embraced materialism. If we fight racism, we do it within ourselves. We love peace but don't know how to stop the bomb.

In many ways, we have quietly joined the society we stood apart from and against. We are driving in our fathers' Michelin tracks.

But we also influenced that society. We loosened the rules. We make it okay to be different.

The old roles for men and women, for blacks and for homosexuals have been re-written and new parts have been added. Many corporations have been forced to develop a conscience. The government took steps to clean up the environment. Consumers woke up.

Still, with American politics trying to take us backward, it would be wonderful to have Lennon around writing music to keep us sane. But we are on our own now. We are all starting over.

THE LENNON SOUND

*Eve Zibart, The Washington Post, Washington, DC,
December 10, 1980*

*"They were doing things nobody was doing. Their chords
were outrageous, just outrageous, and their harmonies made it
all valid... Everybody else thought they were for the teenyboppers, that they were gonna pass right away. But it was obvious to
me that they had staying power. I knew they were pointing the
direction where music had to go."*

Bob Dylan to biographer Anthony Scaduto

John Lennon helped alter forever the vernacular of pop
culture.

As the driving artistic *personality* of the Beatles—sharp,
sardonic, even savage—Lennon ignited a bonfire of conventional craft and concept that leveled the pop establishment.

He lit it with an urgency of delivery, a bright, sometimes
brittle lyric sweep, a powerful rhythm and a refusal to pamper
either the pop forms he was stretching or the rock themes he
was articulating.

In the early '60s, rock 'n' roll emerged as not so much a
compound of idioms—rhythm and blues and rockabilly and
pop and do-wop and dance band—as a kind of mutation, a
spontaneous generation of frustration and desire and rever-
berant exultation. Lennon and McCartney gave it depth, incor-
porating classical strains, gospel, country. They admired
Muddy Waters and Howling Wolf and Chuck Berry and Little
Richard and Elvis and Buddy Holly. They added a string quintet
to "Eleanor Rigby" and Beethoven's Ninth to "Yellow Submarine." They had a compelling sense of the arresting chord
progression, the contrapuntal bass line, the lyric delivery.

Lennon was no guitar wizard. Early on, Ringo said, "I can
only play on the off beat because John can't keep up on the
rhythm guitar." Lennon himself said, "I consider myself a
primitive musician just because I never studied music."

He didn't consider his songwriting primitive: "I had a sort
of professional songwriter's approach to writing pop songs... I
was already a stylized songwriter on the first album... Then I

started being me about the songs, not writing them objectively but subjectively."

In the mid-'70s, Lennon described a kind of evolution in his technique: "Dylan was always saying to me, 'Listen to the words, man!' and I said, 'I can't be bothered. I listen to the sound of it, the sound of the overall thing.' Then I reversed that and started being a words man. I naturally play with words anyway, so I made a conscious effort to be wordy a la Dylan. But now I've relieved myself of that burden and I'm only interested in pure sound."

As a folk hero, Lennon personified that blending of social and cultural and political ideals that characterized the '60s. It was a *trompe l'oeil* effect, and the increasing fragmentation and ultimate splintering of the Beatles themselves presaged their followers' confusion.

In even his most raucous numbers, Lennon cajoled his constituency to peaceful ends. And throughout the '70s, with Yoko Ono, Lennon pled for peace. Ono and Lennon began their marriage with a lie-in for peace. *All we are saying is give peace a chance.* In their new release, "Double Fantasy," Lennon and Ono celebrate the joys of parenthood and housekeeping and marital fidelity. Musically, it showed little trace of the aggressively innovative composer Lennon was once; philosophically, the trail was clear.

Lennon's total influence is incalculable. He left his mark not only on Top 40 radio but, rippling outward, on Muzak and Boston Pops and commercials and ballet and fashion and makeup and graphic arts and slang and recreational drugs and Broadway musicals and poetry and children's stories and role models and movie stars and sex and symbolism.

In his preface to a book on the Beatles, composer Leonard Bernstein said that Lennon and McCartney "embodied a creativity mostly unmatched in that fateful decade."

"Ringo was a lovely performer and George a mystical, unrealized talent," Bernstein wrote. "But John and Paul, Saints John and Paul, were, and made and aureoled and beautified and eternalized the concept that shall always be known, remembered and deeply loved as the Beatles."

WRITING THE SCORE FOR A GENERATION

Sheila Hershow, Federal Times, Washington, DC,
December 29, 1980

All we were saying was give peace a chance. But until John Lennon gave us the words, we never managed to say it right.

We chanted, and the chants were studded with obscene words, and older Americans, frightened and repelled by those words, never listened to what we were saying. Or we burned American flags, an ugly, ill-chosen gesture that was perceived as an assault on the country so many of us were trying to save. And maddened and misunderstood, some of us grew violent.

John Lennon gave us nine words that could not be misinterpreted. Nine words that could not be misheard as a cry for communism or immorality or drugs or destruction. All we are saying, we said, is give peace a chance.

And, at his best, Lennon gave us the attitude—sane, unpompous, irreverent but caring, self-deflating but not self-hating, undefeated, bright and whacky—that helped us survive the viciousness of the late 1960's and early 1970's. "It's a fool," sang the Beatles, "who plays it cool by making the world a little colder."

Lennon was so likable in "A Hard Day's Night," a contemporary Groucho, the Peter Pan leader of a pack of lost boys on the run from love-crazed fans, greed-crazed exploiters, a humorless press and their own inescapable superfame. He was brash and he was bratty but he was never surly or stupid. He was, as the English say, "too clever by half."

The Beatles' songs were peopled by the life-starved Eleanor Rigby "wearing a face that she keeps in a jar by the door," the manic, dauntless "paperback writer," and the "real nowhere man" who was, of course, "a bit like you and me." There was the "holy roller" with the "ju-ju eyeballs" and the pre-Women's Movement "girl" who left her lover because "she could never be free" while he was around. Prophetically, there was the mindlessly murderous Maxwell whose "silver hammer" came down upon the heads of his victims until he was "sure that they were dead."

MINSTREL EXTRAORDINAIRE

M.S. Harris, Local, Cornwall, NY, December 10, 1980

He's gone.

More than just a feeling of emptiness and terrible shock followed the news of the violent death of John Lennon on Monday.

For anyone who grew up loving The Beatles, the sense of loss was almost sickening. Not just for the music created by John Lennon and The Beatles, but for the philosophy of brotherhood which Lennon preached so eloquently, and simply, in his lyrics.

This writer was an adolescent when The Beatles rocked the world with their "long" hair and innovative music. As The Beatles grew and changed, so did millions of young people throughout the world.

With John Lennon as their prime mover, The Beatles created waves in the mid- and late 1960s. "All we are saying, is give peace a chance," sang John Lennon.

Imagine a world, he wrote and sang, where there's no hatred, or war, or defined countries, or religion, or possessions. Imagine a world where people live as one, he sang.

While one might not accept all of his philosophies, perhaps, the importance of his voice in this world—a voice which asked us to question some of the basic pre-conceptions of society in the 20th century—was immense.

One didn't have to agree with John Lennon all the time to appreciate the reality that he asked people to have an open mind about possibilities of the way we live and treat each other.

His senseless murder leaves us numb.

"All you need is love," he told us.

And that's what he gave.

WHY SOME WEPT FOR JOHN LENNON

Andy Rooney, Chicago Tribune, Chicago, IL, December 21, 1980

A young man I like came into the office the other morning and I happened to be walking past the coatrack when he was fumbling with a hanger.

"Good morning," I said.

As if I had asked him how he felt, he said, "I feel terrible about this thing."

His eyes were red and tears came to them again as he turned and hung up his coat. What moved him was the murder of John Lennon.

I walked back to my office and got thinking about how little it had moved me. I felt no real sadness, only interest in it as a news story and anger over its violent nature.

I had closed my mind to the Beatles. They were a phenomenon I had been exposed to a thousand times but they never interested me much. I liked some of their music, but I'm a musical ignoramus and didn't really appreciate how technically good they were. Nor did I get much meaning from the words of their songs. I thought they confused obscurity with depth.

Part of my negative feeling about the Beatles came not so much because I never bothered to appreciate their music but because I thought they had made drugs look attractive to a whole generation. Many of their songs seemed to me to be invitations to go fly with them. The "Yellow Submarine" was made to look like an attractive trip for young people to take.

My young office friend's genuine sorrow made it clear to me that I'd missed something. And in the days since John Lennon's death, I've read and heard a lot more about him. I feel a lot worse now than I did the night I heard he'd been shot. No amount of reading about or listening to Elvis Presley would make me feel anything different about him, but Lennon was out of Presley's class as a musician and as a human being.

It is apparent that Lennon had been trying desperately, and with a lot of success, to live his way out of what he got himself into by being a Beatle. He wasn't rejecting everything that had meant to him. He was just saying it was over and he wanted to move on to something else. It was something he didn't want to be anymore and a lot of people weren't satisfied to let him stop being it. The man who shot him was one of them.

Whatever Lennon was as a Beatle, he'd obviously been something different for the last five years. He said he liked to stay home and bake bread and take care of his 5-year-old son. It is obvious that he was sincere. He said it not to create an effect on the minds of readers of that statement but because that's honestly what he wanted to do.

Almost everyone who becomes famous ends up acting the way famous people act. It isn't so much that famous people want to act that way; they are forced into certain patterns of behavior. John Lennon was trying to act some way other than the way famous people act and people wouldn't let him. Most of all, his murderer wouldn't let him.

It's very sad and I understand now my friend's tears.

FANS GRIEVE FOR LENNON AT VIGILS

Joseph Berger, Newsday, Long Island City, NY, December 15, 1980

"Come together...over me," he had sung. And yesterday in Central Park, perhaps 100,000 strong, they came together over John Lennon—the generations that had been touched by his music and spirit and now wanted to mourn his death with one communal release of emotion.

There were women pushing baby carriages who had shrieked for the Beatles as teenyboppers, graying flower children still clinging to Lennon's vision of a world of love and peace, teenagers whose toddler innocence had been charmed by the frolics of the "Yellow Submarine" cartoon, and grandmothers who had once scolded their children for listening to subversive Beatles messages that they later grew to like.

The same scene was repeated around the nation and the world—in Chicago, Los Angeles, Boston, Philadelphia, Seattle, Baton Rouge, Salt Lake City, Miami, Toledo, and Melbourne, Australia—by perhaps millions of Lennon's fans. In Nassau County, about 500 persons, young and old, gathered at Eisenhower Park for 10 minutes of silence. In Liverpool, a seven-hour memorial concert that drew 30,000 was disrupted by a hysterical rush to the outdoor stage because a band had started playing non-Beatles numbers. About 100 persons suffered injuries, nearly all of them minor, and some fainted—but the concert resumed.

In all of those places, they came together because Lennon's widow, Yoko Ono, deciding against a funeral, had asked Lennon's fans to join instead in a silent vigil of 10 minutes at 2 PM yesterday—"wherever you are." During the vigil, Ono remained in seclusion in her Dakota apartment building at 1 West 72nd Street, only a short walk from the Central Park band shell, where the New York vigil was held.

Some came to Central Park with flowers in their hair, some with flaming candles. Some wore commemorative T-shirts and buttons, and carried radios tuned to his music. Many carried pictures of Lennon—the fresh, guileless face of the Beatles' debut in the United States, the bearded guru of the early '70s, the more thoughtful pose of his last years.

On a chill day under a sky that was alternately soft blue and leaden, they massed on the mall and in the fields in front of the Central Park band shell. On the band shell, a slightly larger-than-life-sized picture of Lennon in his later years had been mounted on an easel set among wreaths of flowers.

First people simply took each other in, took in the great variety of styles and outlooks that Lennon had both attracted and influenced.

Then two walls of loudspeakers began throbbing out his songs, and the crowd listened. When the first notes of "All You Need Is Love" were sounded, there were cheers, and when "Give Peace a Chance" was played, thousands fervently thrust up their fingers in the V-shaped sign of peace.

Then, at precisely 2 PM, in accord with Ono's wishes, a wave of silence swept over the crowd.

It lasted for 10 minutes and was broken only by the flap of helicopter rotors overhead and the crackle of police radios. Many in the crowd sobbed openly. A heavy-set woman with red hair, her hands shielding a flaming candle from the wind, let the tears stream down until her glasses slipped on her nose. Others solemnly bowed their heads, or shut their eyes, or moved their lips in prayer or embraced someone standing nearby.

When the 10 minutes ended, a spray of white balloons filled the air. The speakers broke out in Lennon's song asking people to "Imagine" a world where there's "nothing to kill or die for," where people are "living life in peace." Some who had restrained tears during the silence could do so no longer.

It was part happening and part funeral, at once a joyous remembrance of the verve of the 1960s and 1970s and a lament for lost youth, twisted hopes and, mostly, for the loss of John Lennon.

Many in the Central Park crowd had come wearing the

styles that Lennon fancied throughout the years—the broad-brimmed hats, fringed suede jackets, leather boots, military coats, Greek fisherman's caps. They came with an even greater variety of motives.

The crowd had started gathering at the band shell, on the Fifth Avenue edge of the park near 72nd Street, after dawn. Vic Lauer, a 30-year-old state office worker with long hair and a long, curly beard, had driven with several friends from Allentown, Pennsylvania. "It seemed like the Beatles were always saying and singing the things I was feeling, the frustration and awareness," he said. "The things I felt, nobody else knew about, but they were playing it. It was like having an amplifier to my soul.

"I believe the soul of John Lennon knows what is going on right here," Lauer said. "I want him to know by the outpouring across the land that we feel, we really feel, for him. And, through this, he can rest in peace."

ACKNOWLEDGEMENTS

The Editors of Proteus would like to extend many thanks to the following people and publications for their contributions of word and spirit to the memory of John Lennon and this fitting tribute:

Steve Acker, JOHN ONO LENNON. *The Capital Reporter,* Jackson, MS. Reprinted by permission of *The Capital Reporter.*

Art Aguilar, THE WALRUS WAS JOHN. *The East LA Tribune,* Los Angeles, CA. Reprinted by permission of *The East LA Tribune.*

Bill Ashton, LENNON ON RECORD: TWO DECADES. *The Miami Herald,* Miami, FL. Reprinted by permission of *The Miami Herald.*

Clive Barnes, INTELLECTUAL LENNON: SOCIAL REVOLUTIONARY. *The Chicago Sun-Times,* Chicago, IL. Reprinted with author's permission.

Bob Batz, Jr., LENNON DEATH PUTS CLOUD OVER YOUTH. *The Dayton Daily News,* Dayton, OH. Reprinted by permission of *The Dayton Daily News.*

Joseph Berger, FANS GRIEVE FOR LENNON AT VIGILS. *Newsday,* Long Island City, NY. Reprinted by permission © Newsday, Inc.

Denny Boyd, THIS IS ALL ABOUT THE JOHN LENNON I LOST. *The Vancouver Sun,* Vancouver, BC, Canada. Reprinted by permission of *The Vancouver Sun.*

Al Carter, A LOT OF PEOPLE WERE CRYING. *The Daily Oklahoman,* Oklahoma City, OK. Reprinted by permission of *The Daily Oklahoman.*

President Jimmy Carter, statement, attributed.

Russ Christian, LENNON REMEMBERED FOR MORE THAN HIS MUSIC (Letter to the Editor). *The San Jose Mercury,* San Jose, CA. Reprinted by permission of *The San Jose Mercury.*

Jay Cocks, THE LAST DAY IN THE LIFE. *Time* Magazine, New York, NY. Reprinted by permission © *Time* Magazine.

Ray Connolly, THE SURREAL GENIUS OF ROCK. *Liverpool Daily Post,* Liverpool, England. Reprinted by permission of *Liverpool Daily Post.*

Richard Dyer, WITHIN HIS MUSIC. *The Boston Globe,* Boston, MA. Reprinted by permission of *The Boston Globe.*

Ellen Goodman, THE PROMISE IS GONE. *The Boston Globe,* Boston, MA. © 1980, The Boston Globe Newspaper Company/Washington Post Writers Group. Reprinted with permission.

Sheila Hershow. WRITING THE SCORE FOR A GENERATION. *The Federal Times,* Washington, DC. Reprinted with permission of *The Federal Times.*

Robert Hilburn, JOHN LENNON: NO SECRET INTERIOR, JUST INTEGRITY. *Los Angeles Times,* Los Angeles, CA. © 1980, *Los Angeles Times.* Reprinted by permission.

Robert Huntington, Jr., LOST: ANOTHER GREAT SPIRIT (Letter to the Editor). *The Hartford Courant,* Hartford, CT. Reprinted by permission of *The Hartford Courant.*

Peter Jones, UK COLLEAGUES GENEROUS WITH THEIR TRIBUTES. *Billboard* Magazine, Los Angeles, CA. Reprinted by permission of *Billboard* Magazine.

Faye S. Joyce, STARTING OVER: LIFE WITHOUT JOHN LENNON. *St. Petersburg Times,* St. Petersburg, FL. Reprinted by permission of *St. Petersburg Times.*

Andrew Kopkind, LENNON WITHOUT TEARS. *The SoHo News,* New York, NY. Reprinted with author's permission.

Toni Kornheiser and Tom Zito, LENNON: ALWAYS UP FRONT. *The Washington Post,* Washington, DC. Reprinted courtesy of © *The Washington Post.*

Rabbi Marcus Kramer, EVERYONE SHOULD SPEAK LENNON'S LANGUAGE. *The Staten Island Advance,* Staten Island, NY. Reprinted by permission of *The Staten Island Advance.*

George Melly, JOHN LENNON. *Punch* Magazine, London, England. Reprinted by permission of © *Punch* Magazine (Rothco). All rights reserved.

John Murray, JOHN LENNON'S MUSIC WILL NEVER DIE (Letter to the Editor). *The Denver Post,* Denver, CO. Reprinted with author's permission.

Richard Roberts, YESTERDAY MOURNING BEFORE SUNRISE. *The Philadelphia Evening Bulletin,* Philadelphia, PA. Reprinted by permission of *The Philadelphia Evening Bulletin.*

Andy Rooney, WHY SOME WEPT FOR JOHN LENNON. The Chicago Tribune/ New York News Syndicate, Chicago, IL. Reprinted with author's permission.

Don Short, LIGHTER SIDE OF JOHN LENNON. *Los Angeles Times* Syndicate, Los Angeles, CA. Reprinted by permission of the *Los Angeles Times Syndicate.*